Reading Bridge™

1st grade

Written by:

Carla Dawn Fisher & Julia Ann Hobbs

Project Directors: Michele D. Van Leeuwen
Scott G. Van Leeuwen

Creative & Marketing Director: George Starks

Product Development & Design Director: Dante J. Orazzi

Reading Bridge™
1st Grade

For more information write or call:
Rainbow Bridge Publishing
PO Box 571470
Salt Lake City, UT 84157-1470
801-268-8887
www.rainbowbridgepub.com

Original Cover Art:
Joe Flores

Proofreaders:
Kathleen Bratcher, Dorothy Duckworth, Suzie Ellison, Ben Fulton, Leslee Knutson, Michele Van Leeuwen, Dante Orazzi, Debby Reed, George Starks, Amanda Sorensen

Graphic Design, Illustration and Layout:
Leslee Knutson, Dante Orazzi, Amanda Sorensen

Special Thanks:
Dr. Leland Graham

For updates, corrections and changes please log on to www.rbpbooks.com

Printing History:
First Printing 2000

ISBN: 1-887923-52-7

Printed in the United States of America
10 9 8 7 6 5 4 3 2

Table of Contents

Introduction

The **Reading Bridge** series is designed to improve and motivate students' reading. This book has been developed to provide first grade students practical skill-based exercises in the areas of inferences, main ideas, cause and effect, fact and opinion, and figurative language. The purpose of this book is to familiarize students with the kinds of reading tasks they will encounter on a daily basis. Furthermore, reading will enrich and facilitate their lives as young adults in an ever-changing world that has information readily available, but only if they learn to take advantage of and appreciate reading.

The stories, poems, essays and puzzles in this collection are each accompanied by exercises that address reading skills. Each story, poem or essay has been written so that students at the first grade level can read it successfully. The carefully thought-out questions will help your students learn to think, inquire, create, imagine, respond and, in some instances, do research to learn more about a specific topic.

Reading Bridge adapts to any teaching situation whether at home or in the classroom. It can be used in many different ways. For instance:

- ✔ **For at-home practice:** this series is ideal to supplement or extend school work and home-school reading programs.
- ✔ **For the entire class:** this series can be used for intensive reinforcement of reading skills or to simply supplement a Basal Reading Program.
- ✔ **For reading groups:** this series will provide skills practice at appropriate levels, and the reading exercises become progressively more challenging.
- ✔ **For individual use:** this series will help build a completely individualized program.

Use Your Dictionary!!!

The English language is made up of thousands and thousands of words, so many words that it would be impossible for you to know what every single one of these words means! But wait! Just because you come across a word in this book, or somewhere else, that may be unfamiliar to you, does not mean that you should ignore it or give up on learning its meaning.

Instead, use a dictionary to learn the meaning of the word you don't know. You'll get better scores on the exercises in this book. More importantly, you'll expand your knowledge base and become a better communicator because you'll be able to both express yourself and understand other people more clearly!

Dic • tion • ar • y, n. 1. a book of alphabetically listed words in a language, with definitions, pronunciations, and other information about the words.

1st Grade Reading List

Ackerman, Karen

Song and Dance Man

Ahlberg, Janet

Funnybones

Allard, Harry

Miss Nelson is Missing

Andersen, Hans Christian (retold by Anne Rockwell)

The Emperor's New Clothes

Arnold, Tedd

No Jumping on the Bed

Brown, Marcia

Stone Soup: an Old Tale

Cohen, Barbara

Molly's Pilgrim

Cosgrove, Stephen

Leo the Lop—I, II, III

Hucklebug

Morgan and Me

Kartusch

Snaffles

Dicks, Terrance

Adventures of Goliath

Duvoisin, Roger

Petunia

Veronica

Freeman, Don

Corduroy

Grimm, Jacob

The Frog Prince

Hall, Donald

Ox-Cart Man

Hutchins, Pat

Don't Forget the Bacon!

Good Night Owl!

Rosie's Walk

Isadora, Rachel

My Ballet Class

Kellogg, Steven

Paul Bunyon, A Tall Tale

Leaf, Munro

The Story of Ferdinand

Wee Gillis

1st Grade Reading List

Lobel, Arnold

Frog and Toad series

McCaughrean, Geraldine

Saint George and the Dragon

McCloskey, Robert

Make Way for Ducklings

Minarik, Else Holmelund

Little Bear

Peet, Bill

The Ant and the Elephant

Big Bad Bruce

Buford, the Little Bighorn

The Caboose Who Got Lose

Jethro and Joel Were a Troll

Schwartz, Alvin

In a Dark, Dark Room

Sendak, Maurice

Higglety, Pigglety Pop!

Sharmat, Marjorie Weinman

Nate the Great and the Musical Note

Slobodkina, Esphyr

Caps for Sale

Steig, William

Gorky Rises

Roland, the Minstrel Pig

Viorst, Judith

Alexander and the Terrible, Horrible, No Good, Very Bad Day

Waber, Bernard

Ira Sleeps Over

Ward, Lynd

The Biggest Bear

Yolen, Jane

Picnic with Piggins

Incentive Contract

In • cen'tive, n. **1.** Something that urges a person on. **2.** Enticing. **3.** Encouraging **4.** That which excites to action or moves the mind.

Below, List Your Agreed-Upon Incentive for Each Story Group

Student's Signature ______________________ **Parent, Teacher, or Guardian Signature** ______________________

Place a ✓ after each story & exercise upon completion

Page	Story & Exercise Title	✓
8	Sam and Rab	
10	The Tan Rat	
12	A Big Wig	
14	Pig, Hen and Chicks	
16	Meg, the Vet	
18	Pups and Cubs	
20	I Wish	
22	At the Pond	
24	Pets are Friends	

My Incentive Is

Page	Story & Exercise Title	✓
44	World of Color	
46	Hide and Seek	
48	The Ranch	
50	Wild Animals for Benjamin	
52	Sampson the Robot	
54	Barney Bear	
57	Aunt Jenny's Forest	
60	What's in a Cake?	
62	Garden Mouse and House Mouse	

My Incentive Is

Page	Story & Exercise Title	✓
26	Josh's Backpack	
28	It's Time	
30	Move, Dance, Follow	
32	The Shipmate	
34	Quiet Time	
36	Boats and Acorns	
38	Firemen Know	
40	What's for Lunch?	
42	Space Travel	

My Incentive Is

Page	Story & Exercise Title	✓
65	Camp Sage	
68	Backyard Camping	
71	Little Toad	
74	Gardens	
77	Janet the Zookeeper	
80	"Sea" What You Can See	
83	Did You Know?	
86	Grandma's Dinner	
88	Mighty Dragons	

My Incentive Is

Sam and Rab

Sam has a tan cat.

Rab is Sam's cat.

Sam has a cap and a hat.

Rab can pat Sam's cap.

Sam has a bag and a bat.

Sam can tap the bat.

Rab ran at the bag and sat.

Rab naps and naps on the bag.

Name ....

READING CHALLENGE

After reading "Sam and Rab," answer the following questions.

1. In the story there are six words that rhyme with mat. Write four of them.

__________ __________ __________ __________

2 What is the name of Sam's cat? ____________________

3. Name four other things listed in this story that Sam has.

__________ __________ __________ __________

4. Name another word that rhymes with:

bag ___ag   tap ___ap   tan ___an

5. Why did Rab run at the bag? ____________________

____

6. Draw a picture of Sam and Rab.

Total Correct ________

The Tan Rat

Tax is a fat tan rat.

Tax has Pam's hat.

Bad Tax.

Pam ran after the tan rat.

Tax ran and ran.

Tax ran in a can past the man.

Tax naps in the can.

The man ran to nab the rat. Zap!

The man can nab the fat tan rat in the can.

Pam has the hat.

Pam taps the rat in the can that the man has.

Can Tax, the tan rat, nap? No!

Name ....

Reading Challenge

After reading "The Tan Rat," answer the following questions.

1. What are some words that rhyme with Tax?

   ____

2. What does Tax have that belongs to Pam? ____________________

3. Why did Tax run? ____________________

4. What color is the rat? ____________________

5. Where did the rat hide? ____________________

6. Who nabbed the rat? ____________________

7. Why couldn't the rat nap in the can? ____________________

   ____

8. What word in the story rhymes with jab? ____________________

9. What do you think the man should do with the rat? ____________________

   ____

   ____

   ____

Total Correct ________

A Big Wig

This is a big wig.

The tan pig has the wig.

Will it fit a tan pig?

Zip, zap!

The thin cat has the wig.

Will it fit a thin cat?

Tip, tap!

The frog sat on the wig.

Will it fit the frog?

Bim, bam!

The big ram has the wig.

Will it fit the big ram?

No! No! No!

Name ....

READING CHALLENGE

After reading "A Big Wig," answer the following questions.

1. What animals are in this story?

________________ ________________

________________ ________________

2. Write a word found in the story that tells something about how these animals look:

pig ________________ cat ________________

ram ________________

3. What color do you think the frog in the story is? ________________

4. Name two words that rhyme with frog. ____________ and ____________

5. Does <u>zip</u>, <u>zap</u> mean fast, slow, or happy? ________________

6. <u>Circle</u> the two words in each row that rhyme.

A. wig	pig	frog	ram
B. pig	ram	fit	bam
C. tip	wig	bit	zip
D. the	thin	pin	cat

7. What word is the opposite of <u>no</u>? ________________

Total Correct ________

Pig, Hen and Chicks

Tim has a big hen and little chicks.

Tim fed the hen and chicks.

Tim fed the hen and chicks in this pen.

The pig ran to the hen and chicks.

The hen and chicks ran and ran.

Tim ran fast after the pig.

The pig ran and ran.

The pig ran past the chicks and hen.

Tim has the hen and chicks.

Tim has the hen and chicks in the pen.

The hen and her chicks nap.

Dad ran after the pig.

Dad has the pig in a sack.

Dad fed the pig in the sack.

The pig naps.

Tim and Dad nap.

Name ....

READING CHALLENGE

After reading "Pig, Hen and Chicks," answer the following questions.

1. **Who has a hen and chicks?** ______________________________

2. **What is something you feed hen and chicks?** ______________________________

____

3 **Who is being bad in this story and why?** ______________________________

____

4. **Where did Tim put the hen and chicks?** ______________________________

____

5. **Cross out the word in each row that does not belong.**

A.	B.	C.	D.
pig	book	ran	little
hen	Tim	sack	big
pen	dad	walk	huge
chicks	mom	jump	giant

6. **In the first line of the story which two words are opposites?**

______________ and ______________

7. **Why did Dad, Tim, pig, hen and the chicks need to nap?** ______________________________

____

8. **What two words in the story rhyme with ten?** ____________ and ____________

Total Correct ________

Meg, The Vet

Meg is a vet that helps pets.
Ross is a pet dog.
Ross fell on his leg.
Call Meg, the Vet.
Can Meg help Ross' leg?
Yes, Meg helps Ross with his leg.
Tip Tom is a pet chick that is sick.
Tip Tom has no pep.
Can Meg the Vet help Tip Tom?
Yes, Meg can help Tip Tom get back his pep.
Tess and Pam are house cats
Tess and Pam play in the house, yard and garage.
Tess and Pam are in a big mess.
Can Meg help them? Yes.
Meg the Vet can help Tess, Pam and pets.

Name ....

READING CHALLENGE

After reading "Meg, the Vet," answer the following questions.

1. **What is a vet? Put an X next to the correct answer.**

   A. ____ a doctor for animals B. ____ a doctor for people

2. **Write two words in the story that rhyme with vet.** __________ **and** __________

3. **What is wrong with Tip Tom?** ______________________________

   ____

4. **Does pep mean that Tip Top has no energy?** ______________________

5. **What kind of a mess do you think Tess and Pam were in?** __________

   ____

6. **Write three of your own words that rhyme with call.**

   ______________ ______________ ______________

7. **Did Meg help everyone in the story that needed her?** __________

   ____

8. **Could Meg help horses and cows? Why or why not?** __________

   ____

9. **Cross out the following words that do not rhyme with Ross.**

   cross toss mess boss guess

Total Correct ________

Pups and Cubs

Pups and cubs are little.

Pups are pets for us.

Cubs are not pets.

Pups run after Tom and Bill.

Tom and Bill run with the pups.

What fun, what fun to run with pets.

The fox runs after the cubs.

The cubs' mom and dad run after the fox.

The fox runs and runs.

That was not fun for the little cubs.

Little pups and little cubs tug.

Pups tug at Nan's rag rug.

Cubs tug and roll on the grass.

Name ....

After reading "Pups and Cubs," answer the following questions.

1. Cubs and pups are babies. What are their mothers called. Draw a line to the answers.

cubs	cat
pups	dog
foal	horse
kitten	bear
calf	cow

2. Why would cubs not be good pets? Put an X next to the correct answer.

_____ **A.** They are toys.

_____ **B.** They are wild animals and need to be free.

_____ **C.** They are children.

3. Who ran with the pups? ______________________________

4. Who ran after the cubs? ______________________________

5. Circle the words that rhyme with:

cubs:	ducks	tubs	rubs
pup:	cup	map	up

6. Why did the cubs' mom and dad run after the fox?

____

7. What are the names of the people in this story? ______________________

____

Total Correct _______

I Wish

I wish, I wish, I wish

I wish I had a fish in a dish.
I wish I had a ring that can sing.
I wish I had a ship for a trip.
I wish I had a fan for the man.
I wish I had a frog on a log.
I wish I had a fox in a box.
I wish I had a hen in a pen.
I wish I had a dog and a hog.
I wish I had chips and dips.
I wish I had socks and locks.
I wish I had yams with ham.
I wish I had a sled and a bed.
I wish I had cubs with tubs.
I wish I had pups and cups.
Mack and Jack wish.
Mom and Tom wish.
I can wish. We all can wish.
What do you wish?

I wish, I wish, I wish

Name

Reading Challenge

After reading "I Wish," answer the following questions.

1. **Write the short vowel words from the story next to each vowel. Write each word one time only.**

   ă ______________________________

   ĕ ______________________________

   ĭ ______________________________

   ŏ ______________________________

   ŭ ______________________________

2. **What do you wish for? Write your story and draw a picture to go with it.**

   ____

   ____

   ____

Total Correct ________

At The Pond

The little ducks and chicks went to the pond. The little ducks went to swim on the pond. Chicks can not swim. The chicks went to the pond to run in the tall grass and to look for bugs.

The pond was wet. The little ducks swam across the pond and back. Then the ducks swam up the pond and back.

The little chicks ran and ran in the tall grass. The chicks ran up the hill and back. The chicks ran across the rocks and back.

"Let's stop and rest," said the ducks. "Yes, let's stop and rest," said the chicks. The ducks and chicks did not have a nest to rest in. The ducks can rest on the pond. The chicks can rest in the grass. So they did.

After the rest on the pond and in the grass, the little chicks were sad. "We miss mom," said the chicks. The little ducks were sad, too. "We miss mom and dad," they said.

The little ducks and chicks went past the pond, past the grass and up the hill. The ducks and chicks went to the nest just for them. They took a nap with the moms and dads in the nests just for them. They napped in the nests.

Ducks can swim. Chicks can not. Ducks can nap in nests just for them and so can the chicks!

Name ....

After reading "At the Pond," answer the following questions.

1. Draw a picture for each of these words.

ducks	chicks
pond	bugs
nests	grass

2. Put a T by the sentences that are true about the story and put an F by those that are false.

_____ **A.** The chicks swam in the pond.

_____ **B.** The ducks swam across the pond.

_____ **C.** The chicks and ducks wanted to rest.

_____ **D.** The ducks rested in the grass.

_____ **E.** The chicks and ducks did not miss their moms.

_____ **F.** Chicks and ducks can rest in nests just for them.

Total Correct _______

Pets are Friends

I live far away from my friends. I <u>rarely</u> get to see them. We do talk to each other on the phone almost every day. At times I am very lonely but most of the time I have fun with a different set of friends, here at my home.

My pony, Sandy, is one of my best animal friends. Some times we ride together to the lake. I pack a sandwich and chips for me. I always make sure that I have carrots and apples for Sandy. They are his favorite.

Last Monday, Sandy and I rode nine miles to the local store and then back nine miles. While we were there, the lady at the store gave me two little pups. I carried them in my arms as Sandy and I rode home. Sandy was very careful as we raced home. He didn't want to knock us off.

Before the summer was over, Lucky and Happy, the two little pups grew into dogs. They went everywhere that Sandy and I went. Now when we go to the lake, I pack a sandwich and chips for me, carrots and apples for Sandy and dog bones for Lucky and Happy. It's like having a party with special friends!

Name ....

READING CHALLENGE

After reading "Pets Are Friends," answer the following questions.

1. Match and combine the words to make compound words. Write these new words.

every stand ______________________

some not ______________________

under where ______________________

can day ______________________

2. Do you think this person in the story lives in the country or the city? __________

3. Does this story tell you the name of the person who has the pets? __________

4. Where did the person in the story get the two puppies?

____

5. What are the names of the puppies? ______________ **and** ______________

6. What does this person take when they go on picnics to the lake?

____

7. In what season does this story take place? ______________________

8. Circle the words in each row that mean about the same.

pups	cats	dogs	horses
big	small	fat	little
books	home	friends	pals
talk	loud	soft	speak

9. In the story rarely means what? Put an X next to the correct answer.

_____ **A.** You see your friends a lot.

_____ **B.** You play with friends every day.

_____ **C.** You don't see your friends a lot.

Total Correct _________

Josh's Backpack

Josh has a brand new backpack. It is dark blue and bright red. He put his best books in it. Next he put his biggest box of crayons in. He put his soccer team picture and their first place cup in. "I don't want to leave my soccer ball out," Josh thought, so he pushed it in. "I can't forget our mascot," he said out loud. He stuffed in Thomas Team Tiger. He had just enough room to put in three pencils and a school tablet.

Josh said good-bye to his Mom as he walked out the door. He ran to catch up with his friends walking to school. "I have a new back-pack," he told his friends. "It is just the right size for me," said Josh. "Are you sure?" asked his friends. "Yep," he said.

Josh got to school. He showed his teacher his new backpack. "May I show it for Show n' Tell?" he asked. After the bell rang, Josh's teacher, Mr. Jacobs, said that Josh could show everyone his new backpack. "Wow," they all said, "that really is a nice one." "Yes," Josh said, "it is just the right size for me. It has everything I need and want in it."

Josh showed them each item that he had in it. When he was all finished he asked, "Are there any questions?" "Yes," said Mr. Jacobs, "Where is your lunch box?" "Oh!" replied Josh, "I guess I left it home. There was no room for it anyway!"

Name ....

READING CHALLENGE

After reading "Josh's Backpack," answer the following questions.

1. **Cross off the word that does not belong in each row.**

A. backpack	suitcase	purse	bag	mascot
B. crayons	scissors	pencils	pens	markers
C. lion	teacher	mother	father	friend
D. notebook	tablet	paper	pen	pad

2. **What does "Show n' Tell" mean?** ____________________

____

3. **Name five things Josh put in his backpack.** ____________________

____

4. **What was Josh's teacher's name?** ____________________

5. **What is another word for "Yep?"**

no yes maybe

6. **What had Josh forgotten to put in his backpack?** ____________________

7. **Find a word in the story that begins with each of the letters below. Write the word next to the letters. If there is more than one, choose just one. If there are no words, leave that space blank.**

A. ________	**B.** ________	**C.** ________
D. ________	**E.** ________	**F.** ________
G. ________	**H.** ________	**I.** ________
J. ________	**K.** ________	**L.** ________
M. ________	**N.** ________	**O.** ________
P. ________	**Q.** ________	**R.** ________
S. ________	**T.** ________	**U.** ________
V. ________	**W.** ________	**X.** ________
Y. ________	**Z.** ________	

Total Correct ________

It's Time

It's time for what?
It's time for time!
Whatever is time for?

It's time to go to bed.
It's time to get up.
It's time to eat.

It's time to be good.
It's time to do your best.
It's time to learn.

It's time to go out.
It's time to come in.
Out or in, it's time to be there.

It's time to grow up.
It's time to stay young.
Whatever your age, it's time.

It's your time to be.
It's my time for me.
Let's be friends, it's time.

Name ________________

READING CHALLENGE

After reading "It's Time," answer the following questions.

1. **Write three words that rhyme with time.**

   ________________ ________________ ________________

2. **In the poem, it says "it's time to eat." What time do you eat these meals during the day?**

   breakfast ________________ lunch ________________

   dinner ________________ snacks ________________

3. **Write the opposite word for the following words. The words are in the story if you need some help.**

   in ____________ stay ____________ here ____________

   worst ____________ old ____________ you ____________

   down ____________ stop ____________ bad ____________

4. **How do you measure time? See if you can name three ways!** ____________

   ____

   ____

5. **What do you do with your time?** ________________________________

   ____

   ____

   ____

   ____

   ____

Total Correct ________

Move, Dance, Follow

My friend and I like to play "Follow the Leader" with our friends at school. When we are home, there's only the two of us, so we just call our game, "Move Like Me."

One day, we were outside playing "Move Like Me" when we started watching the animals. We watched the horses prance. We pranced like the horses. It was kind of like dancing. We watched the dogs chase each other. We moved like the dogs, chasing each other in a circle. We saw ducks waddling and quacking around the barnyard. We did the duck dance and quacked in time to the music. The lambs frolicked past us. We joined them doing the lamb frolicking dance. "Halt," I said, "make way for the mother hen and her five little chicks." They pecked at the dirt for seeds as they tip–toed past us. We quietly joined the chicks, doing the pecking and tip–toe dance. Next, we creepy–crawled with the sluggish bugs in the tall grass.

When we went to school on Monday, we showed our friends our new game. They liked doing it. We play it almost everyday at recess.

"What's it called?" they wanted to know. We said, "It's called, 'Move, Dance, Follow'!"

Name ....

After reading "Move, Dance, Follow," answer the following questions.

1. **Pranced is a moving word. Write four other moving words that are found in this story?**

    ____________________ ____________________

    ____________________ ____________________

2. **What day did the children show their new game to their friends?** __________

    ____

3. **Number the sentences in the order that they come in the story.**

    _____ We watched dogs chase each other.

    _____ We watched the horses prance.

    _____ We creepy crawled with the bugs.

    _____ We frolicked like the lambs.

    _____ We called our game, "Move, Dance, Follow."

4. **Put these <u>ing</u> words in alphabetical order.**

A. watching	__________	**B.** doing	__________
quacking	__________	waddling	__________
playing	__________	pecking	__________
dancing	__________	chasing	__________

5. **<u>C</u> has two sounds. It can sound like <u>s</u>, as in <u>city</u> (soft sound) or it can say <u>k</u>, like in <u>cake</u> (hard sound). Put a <u>circle</u> around the <u>soft</u> <u>c</u> words and cross out the <u>hard</u> <u>c</u> words. One word has both a <u>hard</u> and a <u>soft</u> <u>c</u> in it.**

call	school	prance	cave
dance	can	candy	cell
ducks	recess	cinder	circle

Total Correct __________

The Shipmate

James' Uncle Nate has a sailboat. The name of Nate's boat is "Ride With the Wind." It is the same name that Grandpa Jacobs used for his boat. James is Nate's shipmate. James keeps the boat clean and neat. He washes the deck with soap and water. He beats the sails with brushes and brooms. He checks for rust. He treats it with a chemical that is made just for rust problems.

Nate and James keep track of the weather. They listen for the weather forecast so they will know when it is safe to take the boat out on the water. They like to go fishing in their spare time. James always checks to see if the fishing poles are in good shape. He checks on the fishing reels and the rest of the fishing tackle that they will need to fish with.

James and Nate catch a big wave and the wind! Out they sail! Nate raves about the perfect day they are having, when out-of-the-blue it starts to rain.

The lake is no longer safe. The wind seems to scream, "You had better race to shore." James is brave as he helps his Uncle Nate sail his boat back to shore. Uncle Nate hugs James. He says, "You are the best shipmate I have ever had. You are a keeper."

Name ....

After reading "The Shipmate," answer the following questions.

1 **Who are the main characters in the story?** ______________________________

____

2. **Where does the story take place?** ______________________________

____

3. **Unscramble the words and write them under the correct vowel. If you need help the words are found in the story.**

wokn	teaN	obta	imte
erkpree	sdue	mJsae	asil
aetn	edir	elub	posa

Long $\bar{a}$	Long $\bar{e}$	Long $\bar{i}$	Long $\bar{o}$	Long $\bar{u}$
________	________	________	________	________
________	________	________	________	________
________			________	

4. **What does Uncle Nate mean when he told James, "You are a keeper?"**

____

____

Total Correct ________

Quiet Time

We have always had quiet time in our home. "What do you do during quiet time?" you ask. When I was just little, quiet time was not hard for me. I usually slept right through it. As I got a little older, I used to look at picture books and color.

When I learned to read, quiet time was filled with books. I read real stories and make-believe stories. Real stories are called fact, and make-believe stories are called fiction, I learned. I read stories about animals. I read about jungle animals and zoo animals. I read one on how to take care of pets. I read about strange and unusual animals. There are animals everywhere. If you get tired of animals you can read about plants, outer space, countries, and children everywhere. You can read about anything in the world.

Quiet times are good times to think about your day. It's a time to dream about what you want to be when you grow up. It's a time to use your imagination, to plan all the places you want to visit. Quiet time is a time to think of all the beautiful things we have around us.

Quiet time is over too soon when you don't have time to think because you get too busy growing. I think grown-ups need quiet time, too!

Name ....

Reading Challenge

After reading "Quiet Time," answer the following questions.

1. One of the following sentences is not true about this story. Put an X in front of the one that is not true.

_____ Quiet time can be for taking a nap.

_____ I can read about animals during quiet time.

_____ Quiet time is a good time to think.

_____ Quiet time is at night when everyone is asleep.

2. Are these words spelled correctly? If they are not, write them the correct way. You need to find and spell five words. If you need help, look in the story.

belive	___________	fiction	___________	think	___________
zoo	___________	strenge	___________	outir	___________
animels	___________	quiet	___________	dreem	___________

3. Fill in the blanks. Use one of the words at the end of the sentence.

A. Some stories are ___________ or fiction. (fact, fat, follow)

B. Quiet time is over too ___________. (moon, tune, soon)

C. I read about jungle ___________. (animals, trees, bugs)

D. At our house we have a ___________ time. (quack, loud, quiet)

E. The person in this story thinks that ___________ should have quiet time, too. (animals, plants, grown-ups)

Total Correct ________

Boats and Acorns

Garn and Ellen made some boats. They made them out of wood and paper. Garn's was blue. Ellen's was green. They had a lot of fun with their boats.

They took their boats to the park to sail on the pond. Both boats could float on the water. Garn and Ellen put a load of acorns on each boat to see if they could still sail. They did very well.

"What else can we sail on our boats?" asked Ellen. "Let's get some small rocks and see if that will work," said Garn. They ran off to look for some small rocks. They left their boats on the shore.

Along came two little bushy–tailed squirrels. They spied the acorns on the green and blue wooden sailboats. "Nuts!" they cheered as they made a dash toward the boats. They took as many nuts as they could carry and dashed to their home in an old oak tree. There they stored the acorns and went back for more.

They reached the pond and started to gather more of the nuts when a single gust of wind came up. The breeze shook the boats loose. The sailboats, acorns and squirrels floated out on the water.

The squirrels looked around. "This is fun," they said to each other. They each took an acorn to munch on. "Wow, lunch on a boat!" they chattered. Garn and Ellen returned to find the squirrels floating on the boats in the water. "Nobody's going to believe this," said Garn and Ellen. We should have a camera to take a picture!

Name ....

READING CHALLENGE

After reading "Boats and Acorns," answer the following questions.

1. **Who said the following things in the story?**

______________________ "Wow, lunch on a boat!"

______________________ "What else can we sail on our boats?"

______________________ "Nuts!"

______________________ "Let's get some small rocks and see if that will work."

______________________ "This is fun."

2. **Write the missing vowels in the following words:**

b__ __ts	f___n	l__ __k	m___de
r___cks	m___re	gr__ __n	b___sh

3. **Why do squirrels store nuts and acorns? Put an X next to the correct answer.**

_____ just to have something to do

_____ to eat in the winter

_____ to have a party and invite their friends

_____ to play catch with

4. **What color were the boats?** ______________________

5. **What did the children use to make the boats?**

____

6. **Make a guess. How many small rocks do you think Ellen and Garn could have put on the boats?** ______________________

Total Correct ________

Firemen Know

Some firemen came to our school. They talked to us about the dangers of playing with matches or fire.

They told us about two children who were playing with matches and accidentally caught a haystack on fire. The haystack caught a barn on fire and almost burned the animals in the barn. The grown-ups got the animals out just in time. The bad thing was that the children got scared and tried to put the fire out themselves. Both of them ended up in the hospital with awful burns on their bodies. It took a long time for them to get better.

The firemen told us that if we ever caught on fire, we should stop, drop and roll. They said that if we stop, drop and roll, the fire on us should go out.

"If you are in a burning house, you need to have a plan," said the firemen. They told us to go home, talk to our family and to come up with a fire plan. I did just that and I'm glad I did. Not too long after our fire lesson, we had a fire in our home. We stuck to our plan and we all got out safely!

Thank you, firemen, for teaching us about fire!

Name ....

READING CHALLENGE

After reading "Firemen Know," answer the following questions.

1. Put an X next to the correct answer.

A. When someone comes to your school to talk to everyone it is called an

_____ party. _____ assembly. _____ a get together.

B. What is a haystack?

_____ a stack of hay that cows can eat

_____ a stack of straw for cows to sleep on

_____ a stack of bricks

C. In this story accidentally means

_____ you plan to do something.

_____ you work hard to get something done.

_____ something just happens without making it happen.

2. What is the main idea of this story? Put an X next to the correct answer.

_____ Firemen want us to play with matches.

_____ Being safe from fire.

_____ Being safe in your home.

3. Stop, drop and roll means (Put an X next to the correct answer.):

_____ Stop what you are doing, fall to the ground or floor and roll around.

_____ Stop at a friend's house and drop in.

_____ Roll down a hill covered with grass.

4. Make each one of these words singular by writing the words again, making them mean just one.

animals __________ matches __________ children __________

5. Have you ever had to go to the hospital because you were hurt while doing something or because you were sick? Write or tell about it. If you haven't had to go, write about someone you know who has.

____

____

Total Correct _______

What's for Lunch?

"Mom, what's for lunch?" I yelled as I came in the door. I yelled again. Nobody answered. I went into each room of the house. I even checked out the garage and the back yard. "Nobody's home!" I exclaimed to myself. "I'm hungry, really hungry."

"It looks like whatever is for lunch depends on me," I decided. I looked in the fridge. I took out some lunch meat, lettuce, salad dressing, butter, mustard and cheese. "This will make a great sandwich," I thought. "What, no bread? No bread, no sandwich. Look again," I said to myself.

"You have probably noticed, I have a habit of talking to myself," I said to no one in particular, "I do it all the time."

"I know, I'll scramble some eggs and put ketchup on them. I love eggs. Yes, that's what I'll do. I could eat eggs three times a day. What, you are kidding me, no eggs either? Well, what is there left to have?" I asked.

I was getting desperate and said loudly, "How about some soup? All right! We have chicken noodle, tomato, bean with bacon and vegetable soup. Maybe I'll have chicken noodle."

While I was looking for a can opener, Mom came home carrying sacks of groceries. You guessed it. She had bread, eggs and a bunch of other groceries. She said, "I'm hungry, really hungry. What's for lunch?"

Name ....

Reading Challenge

After reading "What's for Lunch?" answer the following questions.

1. Who did the person in the story find at home?

____

2. Fill in the blanks with words from the story.

A. I'm hungry, ____________ hungry.

B. "Mom, what's for ____________?" I yelled.

C. I know, I'll ____________ some eggs.

D. I was getting ____________.

3. Why didn't the person make a sandwich?

____

4. Why didn't the person scramble some eggs?

____

5. What was the person looking for when Mom came home with the groceries?

____

6. Which kind of soup do you like best? Mark your choice with an X.

_____ tomato _____ vegetable _____ chicken noodle

_____ bean with bacon _____ none of the above

7. Make as many words as you can from the words in the title: What's For Lunch? Try to make at least 10 words.

____________________ ____________________

____________________ ____________________

____________________ ____________________

____________________ ____________________

____________________ ____________________

Total Correct ________

Space Travel

People from the space program are coming to Franklin Elementary School! They are astronauts. They have traveled into space twice and have been involved with others in the space program for a long time. They will tell the students all about their travels and the work they do. Everyone at school is so excited, they couldn't stop talking about it!

The night before the astronauts came, Landon went to bed. He dreamed about being an astronaut. He dreamed that he traveled in a space craft into outer space! He traveled far off the Earth. He landed on Mars and got out of his space craft to explore. He raced in the red clay, making red dust clouds where ever he ran. He traveled around in the rings of Saturn. He went around and around so fast that he got dizzy and spun out of control. Next thing he knew, he was on the floor in his bedroom.

The next day, he was excited to go to school. He listened to all the stories that the astronauts had told. After the astronauts were finished, they asked the children if there were any questions. Landon raised his hand and said, "I don't have a question to ask, but boy do I have a space story to tell!"

Name ....

READING CHALLENGE

After reading "Space Travel," answer the following questions.

1. **Fill in the blank with a word that means about the same as the underlined word. Use the following words:**

   grade ship two thrilled world sailed

   A. The astronauts had been into space ______________ times. <u>twice</u>

   B. The astronauts were coming to Franklin ______________ School. <u>elementary</u>

   C. He traveled off the ______________. <u>Earth</u>

   D. Everyone was so ______________, they couldn't stop talking about it. <u>excited</u>

   E. He dreamed he ______________ in a space ______________ into outer space. <u>traveled</u> <u>craft</u>

2. **Put an <u>X</u> next to the correct answer.**

   A. Landon had a

   _____ picnic. _____ dream. _____ party.

   B. Astronauts travel

   _____ into space. _____ into the ocean. _____ into the earth.

   C. We ask questions to

   _____ tell stories. _____ sleep in bed. _____ learn things.

   D. Mars, Saturn and Earth are

   _____ planets. _____ plants. _____ ice-cream flavors.

3. **Add <u>ed</u>, and <u>ing</u> to these words. Write the words.**

   travel __________ __________ dream __________ __________

   listen __________ __________ finish __________ __________

4. **Would you like to travel into space?** ______________________________

   If so, where would you like to go? ______________________________

   ____

Total Correct __________

World of Color

Look for colors all around.

Everywhere colors can be found.

Green is for grass and fresh peas.

Brown is for bears and trunks of trees.

Red is for roses and valentine hearts.

Black are the words on white reading charts.

Blue is the birds, in the blue sky.

Orange is for oranges, don't ask me why.

Yellow is for bananas, apples and pears.

Colors, all colors, for rocket flares.

Purple cows, I don't think so.

Are pigs pink? I don't really know.

Colorful rainbows can be found.

Look, there are colors all around.

Name ....

READING CHALLENGE

After reading "World of Color," answer the following questions.

1. **List one more thing for each color listed below using your imagination.**

   Green: grass, fresh peas ____________________

   Brown: bears, trunks of trees ____________________

   Red: roses, valentine hearts ____________________

   Black: words ____________________

   White: charts ____________________

   Blue: birds, sky ____________________

   Orange: oranges ____________________

   Yellow: bananas, apples, pears, ____________________

   Purple: ____________________

   Pink: ____________________

2. **Find and write the words in the poem that fit each description listed below:**

   A. contraction ____________________

   B. two long ī words with no i letter ____________________

   C. three words with the ow ou sound ____________________

   ____

   D. a compound word ____________________

3. **Write the base or root word for:**

   colorful ____________________ reading ____________________

   really ____________________ roses ____________________

4. **What is your favorite color or colors? Why?** ____________________

   ____

   ____

Total Correct ________

Hide and Seek

Pete and Jake came over to my home to play with me. We played with my toys for a while. After that we decided to play "Hide and Seek."

We just barely started when my Mom called me, "Randy, Dad can't find his white socks. Will you boys help him look?" We said, "Sure." We looked on the shelf. We looked in boxes and garbage cans. We looked on the floor and the hooks on the wall.

"Here Dad," I called, "we have your socks." "Where did you find them?" asked Dad. "On the coat hooks in the hall," I said. "Thanks," said Dad.

My big sister, Julie, asked, "Randy, have you seen the rag I use to dust with?" "No," I said, "but we will help you look for it."

Pete, Jake and I looked all over for the rag. We found it in the dirty clothes bag. "Here you go, Julie," I said. "Thanks," replied Julie. "It looks like I need to wash it first before I use it."

We went outside to play, just as Mom called, "Randy, I can't find my favorite mixing spoon. Please look for it." "Okay," we said. We found the spoon in the sand pile with all the sand tools. I had used it for a shovel and forgot to put it back. I took it inside. "Here Mom," I said, "I forgot that I had used it and didn't put it back."

Pete and Jake said, "Let's play something else. We are tired of playing Hide and Seek."

Name ____________________

After reading "Hide and Seek," answer the following questions.

1. **Which is the right way to play "Hide and Seek?" Put an X next to the correct answer.**

   _____ **A.** Look for lost things.

   _____ **B.** You hide things and others try to find them.

   _____ **C.** Someone is "It," others hide, and the person who is "It" tries to find them.

   _____ **D.** Everyone goes to the movies.

2. **What did Dad lose?** ____________________

   What did Julie lose? ____________________

   What did Mom lose? ____________________

3. **Write the base or root word for the following:**

playing	______	called	______
decided	______	looked	______
started	______	asked	______
mixing	______	used	______

4. **Is the underlined word in each sentence spelled correctly? Circle yes or no.**

A. Dad lost his <u>whit</u> socks.	Yes	No
B. We <u>loked</u> on the shelf.	Yes	No
C. My <u>big</u> sister, Julie, called me.	Yes	No
D. We <u>found</u> it in the dirty clothes bag.	Yes	No
E. Pete and Jake came <u>ovr</u> to my house.	Yes	No
F. <u>Lets</u> play something else.	Yes	No

Total Correct ________

The Ranch

Dave and Steve live on a ranch in Texas. They have a lot of cattle on their ranch. They have to feed and take care of the cattle.

Dave and Steve must plant a lot of hay and oats for the cattle to eat. The cattle like to eat grass, too. "Don't forget to plant lots of corn," Rafe and Queed chimed in.

Rafe and Queed are ranch hands. They do not own the ranch, but they work there. They live in the bunk house. They have cots to sleep on and a small kitchen to cook in.

Many times they cook on a campfire when they are out on the range. The range is the large area of land around the ranch which the cattle eat from. Rafe and Queed go out on the range and bring the cattle into the corral on the ranch. They have to brand all the new cattle they find, or a calf when it is born.

After the cattle are branded, some of them are taken back out on the range. Some are taken to the cattle market to be sold to other ranchers. Some are taken for meat, to be sold in stores.

Dave and Steve make money for the ranch and themselves by selling the cattle. Rafe and Queed are paid for their work. After all their hard work, Dave, Steve, Rafe and Queed go to town to shop for what they need and want. Dave and Steve buy things to keep the ranch running properly.

Sometimes they go to town to dance and to be with other people. When they go back to the ranch, they are happy, but tired. They are ready to be ranchers again.

Name ....

READING CHALLENGE

After reading "The Ranch," answer the following questions.

1. Match the words that rhyme.

hand	change
go	mother
range	land
cattle	look
other	battle
cook	so

2. Name three things cattle eat. ______________________________,

______________________________ **and** ______________________________

3. Fill in the blanks.

A. Rafe and ______________ are ranch hands.

B. ______________ and Steve live on a ______________ in Texas.

C. Some cattle are ______________ to other ranchers.

4. What do the men on the ranch do for fun?

____

____

5. What is a corral? Put an X next to the correct answer.

______ **A.** a swimming pool for cattle

______ **B.** a field of corn

______ **C.** a place to cook food

______ **D.** a pen for cattle

6. Which two men do not own the ranch? ______________________________

and ____.

Total Correct ________

WILD ANIMALS for Benjamin

Benjamin is my little brother. We call him, Benny, sometimes. He loves wild animals. Whenever we read to him, he always choos-es books that have stories about wild animals. Benjamin's favorite wild animals are bears and buf-faloes. He says that they are strong. He says they are "B" for big, like he is going to be someday.

Our family went on a vacation to Yellowstone National Park in the mountains of Wyoming. We saw a lot of bears and buffaloes there. Benny wanted to get out of the car and pet them. He couldn't understand why Mom and Dad would not let him. They explained how the bears have sharp teeth and claws that can hurt and even kill people. They told him that the buffalo are very strong and get scared easily. When they get scared, they might charge, causing a stampede. This could also hurt and even kill people. Mom told Benny that wild animals do not understand Benny's love for them. She told him they are probably scared of him and feel they have to protect themselves.

We took lots of pictures of the animals for Benny. He loves having them on his bedroom walls. He has a name for each animal in each picture. He pretends that he can talk to them. He pretends that they are his pets. He even makes up stories about them and the fun that they have together.

Benjamin's favorite crackers are animal crackers. Does he eat them? No! He plays with them!

Name ....

Reading Challenge

After reading "Wild Animals for Benjamin," answer the following questions.

1. **Benny's favorite wild animals are ______________________________**

   and ______________________.

2. **Where did he see these animals? ______________________________**

   ____

3. **What did Benny say "B" stands for? ______________________________**

4. **The following words are in the story. Write an opposite word for each one.**
   Use: <u>her</u> <u>weak</u> <u>tame</u> <u>few</u> <u>came</u> <u>dull</u>

   wild ____________ sharp ____________ strong ____________

   him ____________ went ____________ lots ____________

5. **What does pretend mean? Put an X next to the correct answer.**

   _____ **A.** Something that is not real; make-believe.

   _____ **B.** Something that is real.

   _____ **C.** Something that is big and ugly.

6. **Number the following sentences in the order they happened in the story.**

   _____ Benny hung pictures on his bedroom walls.

   _____ The family went to Yellowstone National Park.

   _____ Benny wanted to get out of the car to pet the bears and buffaloes.

7. **What are Benjamin's favorite crackers? ______________________________**

   ____

   ____

Total Correct ________

Sampson the Robot

Sampson is an amazing robot. He was made by Jacob. Jacob and his Dad made Sampson for the Science Fair.

Sampson can dance. Sampson can sing. Sampson can cook, weed the garden and do chores around the house and the yard. Sampson spends most of his time in the backyard.

The most amazing thing about Sampson is that he can read! Sampson loves to read. He loves stories about dragons and dinosaurs. He can't get enough stories about astronauts and space exploration. He reads about children of different lands. He likes to read about where they live, what they wear and what they eat.

One day Jacob left the gate in his backyard open. Sampson wandered out of the yard by himself. When Jacob got home from school, the first thing he did was call for Sampson. When Sampson didn't answer, Jacob looked all over the house for him. He asked his family if they had seen Sampson. They replied, "No, did you look outside for him?"

Jacob went out in the backyard to look for Sampson. He discovered that the gate was open and Sampson was gone!

As Jacob walked down the street looking for Sampson, he asked himself, "Where is the one place that Sampson would want to go?" Sure enough, when Jacob got to the library, there was Sampson sitting among the books. Sampson was reading not just to himself, but to a circle of children.

When Sampson saw Jacob, he called to him, "Jacob, have you ever heard of Little Red Riding Hood?" Jacob smiled and said he had and he sat down to listen.

Name ....

READING CHALLENGE

After reading "Sampson the Robot," answer the following questions.

1. **Who is Sampson?** ________________________________

   Who is Jacob? ________________________________

2. **Name three things Sampson can do.**

   A. ________________________________

   B. ________________________________

   C. ________________________________

3. **What happened when Jacob left the gate open?**

   ____

   ____

4. **Where did Jacob find Sampson?**

   ____

   ____

5. **Match these words with their correct meaning.**

A. space	wonderful
B. astronauts	to find new things or places
C. amazing	open area
D. exploration	answered
E. replied	to hunt for things or places
F. library	people who travel in space
G. discover	a place to find books

6. **Make as many words as you can out of Sampson the Robot.**

   ____

   ____

Total Correct ________

Barney Bear

Barney Bear had a problem. It was winter. He was supposed to be hibernating like the rest of his family, but he was wide awake. "This is not fun," he said out loud, hoping to wake up his mom and dad. "I can't sleep and no one is awake to play with me!"

Barney went outside. "Maybe I can find someone to play with," he thought.

The silent forest was covered with snow. Barney trudged through it carefully. He had never seen snow before since he was normally sleeping during winter! The snow was cold and wet on his paws. "I wonder what this stuff is?" he asked himself. He felt very lonesome. "I guess everyone is asleep. I'm all alone."

He was about to give up trying to find a playmate, when he heard giggling. It was coming from behind some twigs. Barney stepped closer and saw two chipmunks wrestling with each other. "Hello," he called to them. "Well, hello." they shouted, "Aren't you sup-posed to be hibernating?"

"I couldn't sleep," Barney said bashfully. "Do you think I could play with you for a while?" "It's all right with us," the chipmunks said.

Barney met some of the chipmunks' friends. He met Oscar Otter, Oliver Owl, Sally Squirrel and Frankie Fox. Barney and his new friends spent the rest of the day playing in the snow. They made snow forts and had snowball fights. They made snowmen and went sledding. They even flopped on the ground and made snow angels as the sun began to set. Barney was getting very sleepy. "I think I'll go home," he yawned. "Thank you for playing with me." He waved goodbye and returned to his cave. It was dark, warm and quiet inside. He curled up on his bed and fell fast asleep dreaming of his new friends and all the fun things they did.

Name ....

READING CHALLENGE

After reading "Barney Bear," answer the following questions.

1 **What is Barney's problem?** ______________________________

____

2. **Where does this story take place?** ______________________________

____

3. **What does <u>giggling</u> mean? Put an <u>X</u> next to the correct answer.**

_____ talking loudly _____ jumping up and down

_____ laughing _____ whistling

4. **Which animal was not one of Barney's new friends? Put an <u>X</u> next to the correct answer.**

_____ Oliver Owl _____ Frankie Fox _____ John Skunk

_____ Oscar Otter _____ Sally Squirrel

5. **Put a <u>T</u> by the sentences that are true about the story and put an <u>F</u> by those that are false.**

_____ **A.** Bears live in the forest.

_____ **B.** It was winter.

_____ **C.** Bears, otters, owls, squirrels and foxes make snow forts in this story.

_____ **D.** Bears can talk and think like people.

_____ **E.** Bears hibernate in the winter.

_____ **F.** "Thank you" is not a nice thing to say.

6. **<u>Circle</u> the words that mean about the same in each row. These are known as <u>synonyms</u>.**

A. shouted	flopped	yelled	whispered
B. happy	bashful	shy	crying
C. quiet	snow	covered	hushed
D. giggling	hibernating	sleeping	playing

Total Correct _______

Aunt Jenny's Forest

My Aunt Jenny has a home by a forest. She invites my brother and I for visits all the time. In the summertime, I always choose to spend part of my vacation there. I love the tall green trees and the colorful wild flowers. The forest is also home to many insects and animals. I like to explore the forest to see what I can find.

Once my brother, Mark, and I went into the forest together. Mark ran like the wind. The bushes and plants danced and swayed wildly as he flew by. Birds, bees and butterflies were startled by his quick movements. They seemed frantic to get out of his way. Mark chased a rabbit until it escaped into a hole in the forest floor. Mark tried to keep up with a bee as it flew past him. He wanted to find the bee's nest. He darted here and there as he raced on.

I walked quietly along in the forest. There was much to see. I saw a mother deer and her fawn moving about, flicking their tails and their ears. I watched silently as they ran off, deep into the forest. As I turned, I saw a small movement in the tall grass. I discovered a nest full of baby birds. I quietly sat down close by and waited. When the mother bird felt it was safe, she returned with food for her babies. It was so interesting! I watched a long time and then left as quietly as I had come. I did not want to disturb them.

I went back on the path to Aunt Jenny's house. Mark got back way ahead of me. He said, "I had such a good time. What happened to you slowpoke?" I told him about all I had seen. "Next time," he said, "I'm going to be a quiet slowpoke with you."

"Sometime," I promised in return, "I'll run like the wind with you!"

Name ....

READING CHALLENGE

After reading "Aunt Jenny's Forest," answer the following questions.

1. Number the sentences in the correct order that they happened.

_____ I discovered a nest full of baby birds.

_____ Once, my brother, Mark, and I went into the forest together.

_____ I went back on the path to Aunt Jenny's.

_____ Mark tried to keep up with a bee as it flew past him.

_____ My Aunt Jenny has a home by a forest.

2. Circle the correct response. If Mark ran like the wind, he was _____________.

jogging

running very fast

running a little fast

3. What does this person in the story love about the forest? _______________

____

4. What did Mark mean when he said the next time he would be a "quiet slowpoke?"

____

____

5. Circle the long vowel words and put a box around the short vowel words.

close	safe	nest	long
them	told	see	time
left	him	summer	bee
went	wild	way	plant

Total Correct ________

What's in a Cake?

"What's in a cake?" we ask.
Mom says, "It's an easy task."
You need a large mixing bowl, I'm told.
Four beaten eggs will make it all gold.
Flour, vanilla, shortening and milk.
Now beat it until it's as smooth as silk.
Put it in the pan, then into the oven.
Set the heat at three hundred and seven.
We have to sit and wait for it to bake.
Just how long do you think it will take?
Our cake looks good but tastes all wrong.
We must have baked it way too long.

"What's in a cake?" we ask.
Mom says, "It's an easy task."
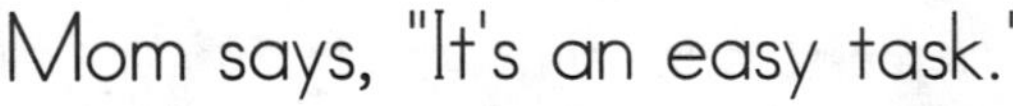

Name ______________________

READING CHALLENGE

After reading "What's In A Cake?" answer the following questions.

1. **Find four sets of words in the poem that rhyme.** ______________________

   ____

   ____

2. **How many eggs go in this cake?** ______________________

3. **What other ingredients go into it?** ______________________

   ____

   ____

4. **Put 1 in front of the sentence that come first in the poem.**
   Put 2 in front of the sentence that happens second.

   A. ________ Now beat it until it's as smooth as silk.

   ________ You need a large mixing bowl, I'm told.

   B. ________ We have to sit and wait for it to bake.

   ________ We must have baked it way too long.

5. **Write the contraction for the following words:**

it is	______________	do not	______________
what is	______________	have not	______________
you are	______________	I am	______________
we are	______________	let us	______________

6. **What is your favorite kind of cake?** ______________________

   What goes into it to make it? ______________________

   ____

   ____

Total Correct ________

Garden Mouse and House Mouse

Once-upon-a-time there were two little mice. They were best of friends. One was a garden mouse, the other, a house mouse. Each one was very happy with where they lived. They would take turns playing in the garden and in the house with each other.

The house mouse lived between the walls in the Jones house. He munched on crumbs and scraps left out on the counters and table. He would nibble a little here and a little there.

The garden mouse lived in the garden under a rock by the gate. He would munch on green beans and cabbage. He would nibble a little here and a little there.

One day the two mice met at the garden gate. They decided to go exploring. They walked out the garden gate and down the road toward the big city. They saw a bus and quickly got on. They arrived in the city. There they met two city mice.

The city mice showed them around the big city. The city mice lived in a large store full of all kinds of food. They all nibbled on fruit and cookies. They nibbled a little here and a little there.

Then they went for a walk through the city. They walked on the sidewalks and across the busy streets. The garden mouse and the house mouse saw many wonderful new things. Before they caught the bus home, they invited the two city mice for a visit. They promised to show them their garden and home. The city mice said they would like to come for a visit very soon.

The two mice arrived home, tired and happy. The garden mouse went to sleep in his home under the rock by the gate. The house mouse went to sleep in his home between the walls. It was a fun day for them.

Name ....

READING CHALLENGE

After reading "Garden Mouse and House Mouse," answer the following questions.

1. **Write M by the sentences that are make-believe and write R by the sentences that are real.**

   _____ A. Mice think and decide to ride on a bus to the city.

   _____ B. A mouse can live in a garden.

   _____ C. Mice nibble on food.

   _____ D. Mice show their friends around the city.

   _____ E. Mice can walk and run.

2. **Write a word from the story that rhymes with the following words:**

   house ____________________ sickly ____________________

   crunch ____________________ beets ____________________

   Gus ____________________ Rome ____________________

3. **Add letters s, es, or change the spelling to make these words mean more than one.**

   bus ____________________ friend ____________________

   mouse ____________________ cookie ____________________

   road ____________________ box ____________________

4. **Why did the garden mouse and the house mouse go to the city?**

   ____

   ____

5. **What does nibble mean? Circle the answer.**

   big bites   medium bites   tiny bites

6. **How long do you think the mice were in the city? Circle the best answer.**

   1 hour   most of one day

   2 days   all of three days

Total Correct ________

Camp Sage

Monica lives in the city. She is nine years old. This is the summer for her to go to Camp Sage. She is not so sure that she wants to go. She does not want to leave her friends. Monica's family says, "Don't worry, you are only going to be gone for five days." "Yes, but that's a long time," she thinks out loud. They all said, "The time will fly by quickly."

The day came for Monica to leave for Camp Sage. She was all packed but not really ready to go. She was still saying, "Five days is just too long to be gone from home."

Monica's parents took her to the camp bus stop where she boarded the bus. Monica sat down and soon she was on her way. She watched as the skyscrapers passed her and the green of the country came into view. She felt that time was not flying by inside the bus, only the outside was fly-ing by.

Later, she arrived at Camp Sage. She was assigned to a tent with three other girls. They unpacked their things, washed up and met at the mess tent, with all the other girls, for dinner. After dinner,

they sat around the camp fire and sang songs. When it was all over, she yawned as she climbed into bed.

The days were spent hiking, fishing, swimming and boating. Three times they got to ride horses along interesting trails. They played volleyball, softball and soccer. The girls played another game where they threw horseshoes. They made different arts and crafts projects using things found around them. They had contests in team sports and other activities.

Before she knew it, Monica and the other girls were packing up their things and boarding the different buses to start for home. Monica said good-bye to all of her new friends. They all promised to write letters and to see each other next year!

The first thing Monica did when she saw her family was to say, "Time really does fly!"

Name ....

THE CROSSWORD CHALLENGE

Camp Sage Puzzle

1									
2				3					

ACROSS

1. Two plus three equals_____________.
2. Another name for a "very tall building."
5. The girls at Camp Sage did arts and ___________________.
6. When you write to someone it is called a __________________.

DOWN

1. "Time flies," means time goes ___________________.
3. A place where there are very few buildings with lots of open spaces is called the ___________________.
4. "To begin something," means to ___________________.

Total Correct ________

Backyard Camping

Brian and Tommy decided to camp out in their backyard. "What do you think we'll need?" Brian asked. "Well, we'll need a tent," Tommy replied, "we'll also need sleeping bags, a flashlight, a radio and some snacks." "Where can we get those things?" Brian asked. "Let's ask Dad," Tommy suggested. "He has a lot of outdoor equipment."

Their dad took them into the garage to find the items they asked for. He managed to find a tent, sleeping bags, a flashlight and the radio.

"You will have to provide your own snacks," he said.

Brian and Tommy dragged the equipment into the backyard. They put the tent up and pulled in the sleeping bags. They put the flashlight inside the tent.

Their Mom made them tuna fish sandwiches. She gave them potato chips, cookies and a bottle of milk. The boys got into their pajamas, took their snacks and went out into the tent.

Backyard Camping, continued

They ate most of their food, listened to the radio and told ghost stories. After that, they fell asleep.

Somewhat later, they heard a rustling outside. "What was that?" Tommy asked. "I don't know!" Brian quaked. The boys sunk down deeper in their sleeping bags as the noise got closer and closer. The next sound they heard was, "meow." It was their cat, Tiger. He had smelled a leftover tuna fish sandwich.

"I thought it was a monster!" laughed Tommy. "Camping is a lot of fun, but it can be scary, too!" laughed Brian. They let the cat in the tent, fed him the leftover tuna fish sandwich and then all three fell asleep.

Name ....

READING CHALLENGE

After reading "Backyard Camping," answer the following questions.

1. **Who are the main characters in this story?** ______________________________

   ____

2. **What did Dad say the boys would have to provide for themselves?** ________

   ____

3. **What did Mom give them to eat?** ______________________________

   ____

4. **What made the boys afraid during the night? Put an X next to the correct answer.**

   _____ ghost stories   _____ Tiger   _____ monsters

5. **The meaning of quaked in this story is (Put an X next to the correct answer):**

   _____ rolled around   _____ loud voice   _____ shaky voice

6. **Fill in the missing letters. The words are found in the story if you need help.**

A.	m___nster	r___di___	bo___ ___le
B.	cam___ing	meo___	f___ash___ight
C.	cl___s___r	ga___age	p___l___ed
D.	san___ ___ich	ba___k___ard	p___t___t___
E.	equip___e___t	de___ide___	pa___am___s

7. **Where did the boys go camping?** ______________________________

   ____

Total Correct ________

Little Toad

Little Toad hopped out of the pond. "Where are you going, Little Toad?" asked all the other toads. "I'm tired of living in this pond with so many toads," he said, "I need more room." With that, Little Toad hopped away leaving all the other toads to wonder why he needed more room.

Little Toad hopped through the tall grass. He came to a fence and squeezed through. On and on he hopped. He met Rabbit along the way. When Little Toad told Rabbit what he needed, Rabbit said, "You can live with me if you want to. I live under the roots of this old tree." "No, thank you," said Little Toad as he hopped away. "I don't think this is the place for me."

Next he met a bee. When he told the bee what he needed, the bee said, "Buzz off. Stay away from me. You cannot live with me in my tree. You would just get stuck in my honey and not be able to get out." Little Toad said, "Don't worry, bee, a honey tree is no place for me." Little Toad hopped away.

Little Toad, continued

Little Toad met a dog. The dog barked and chased him away. Toads and dogs do not belong together, decided Little Toad. Little Toad met a cat, a cow and a horse along the way. They all told Little Toad that he could live with them, but again, Little Toad decided that the places where they lived were not the places for him.

Little Toad hopped here and there. He hopped far away. He found a park. In the park he found a pond! On the pond there were lots of lily pads. On each lily pad there was a frog. There were hundreds of ducks on the pond and several fish under the water. They all said that he could come and live with them. Little Toad tried it for a day and a night. He decided that the pond was more crowded than his old pond at home.

The next day Little Toad hopped on home. The other toads were happy to see him and wanted to know all about what he saw and did. They moved over to make room for him.

Little Toad said, "If you think this place is crowded, you have no idea just how crowded places can be! If I'm going to be among a crowd, I'd just as soon be right here! Anyway, I missed you guys."

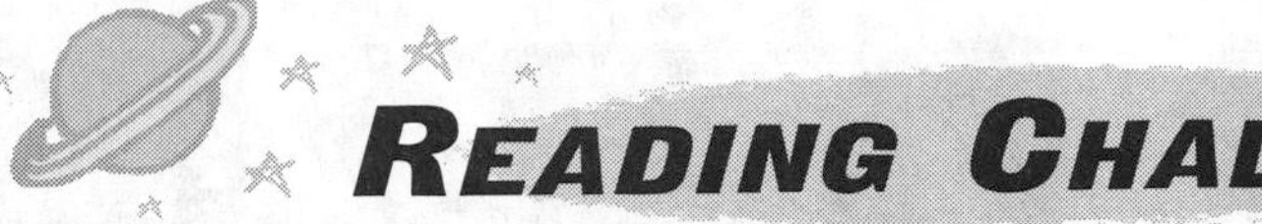

After reading "Little Toad," answer the following questions.

Find the animals in this word search that Little Toad met in the story. Color each word. The words can go across, or up and down. There are 10 animals to find!

l a p o m t o a d s x t j r y i n i o
b f f c g d h e o i k m o a q s u w x
z r l k m o i e g y u z x b a h b y m
w o r a b d j k m n o p q b v w x y z
m g i o v m t s p a b c l i n a v t j
s v t c o w u l i m a d b t f s h i o
r t v a x a c e g i k y p q b l o x m
m k a t b f o x y d u c k s t s r r e
x z y m p q b c a n o s i t u d s f g
s v d j k l u b e e h e a o n c e d p
f o f i s h m u v x s i w z a r c i y

1. **Find one more animal in the word search above.**
   This animal was not named in the story.
   What is the mystery animal? ______________________________

Total Correct ________

GARDENS

My sister, Fran, and I took our pet, Spike, out for a walk. While we were walking, we saw many different gardens.

We saw flower gardens along fences. We saw flowers in pots on people's steps. We looked up and saw flowers in window boxes. We saw flowers in the park on bushes and by the sidewalks. We even saw pink water lilies on the pond. I think that we saw flowers of every color in a rainbow in the gardens we walked by.

As we were walking back home, we saw vegetable gardens. Growing in them were green beans and peas. There were bright red tomatoes and dark, dark, red beets. We saw yellow corn and squash. We saw orange and green carrots. We saw little pumpkins that were green and orange, too. We saw cabbage and onions. There were a few plants that we couldn't name at all. We called them mystery plants. We decided that they might even be weeds. We giggled about that. Mystery weeds!

When Fran and I got home, we locked the gate so Spike couldn't get out. We went in the house where Mom was busy fixing dinner. We wanted to tell Mom about all the different gardens we had seen. She said, "We'll talk about it later." Next we went to talk to Dad. After we told him all about the gardens we had seen, we said, "Dad, do you think that we could have a garden?" Dad said, "Let's discuss it at dinner time."

As we were eating, Dad had us tell about our walk and what we had seen. He told the family we had asked if we could have a garden. Everyone in the family decided that it was a fun idea to have a garden but that it was too late in the season to plant vegetables.

We planted a few flowers in pots for our porch. That night, our family sat down and made plans for next year's planting. We planned on a flower garden and a vegetable garden! Fran and I started saving our money to buy seeds that very night!

Name ....

READING CHALLENGE

After reading "Gardens," answer the following questions.

1. Who is Spike? ______________________________

2. Name three places where the children saw flowers. ____________________

____

3. Which vegetables did the children not see on their way back. Circle them.

corn	peas	potatoes	cabbage
turnips	beets	carrots	parsnips

4 What kind of gardens did the family decide to plant next year? ____________

____

5. Name four long ī words and four long ē words that were in the story.

ī	ē
____________	____________
____________	____________
____________	____________
____________	____________

6. If you could plant a garden, which kind would you plant and what plants would you grow?

____

____

____

____

____

Total Correct __________

Janet, the Zookeeper

Janet has a job. She goes to work everyday. Janet is a zookeeper at Atlas Zoo. Her job is to keep the animals safe and happy.

Janet sees that each animal has plenty to eat and lots of water to drink. Some animals eat seeds and grain. Some do not like seeds and grain. They want meat to eat. Some animals like lettuce, bananas and other fruits and vegetables. Some make a meal of bread. Some find insects and bugs to their liking. Janet makes very sure that each animal gets what they like, as well as what's good for them. She makes sure they sleep well too.

Janet, the zookeeper, watches closely to make sure the animals are healthy. If any of them seem sick or <u>listless</u>, she calls the zoo doctor to check on them. Some animals need vitamins and medicine shots to get better.

Janet checks the animal cages to see that they are kept clean. She sweeps the cages and sprays them with water to clean them. Some animals live in the water. Janet makes sure that the water is clean and at the right temperature for them.

Janet, the Zookeeper, continued

Janet knows that some of the animals like to live where it is warm and that other animals like it to be cold. As a zookeeper, it is her job to take care of this.

Janet wants the animals to be happy. The animals seem to know that Janet is their special helper. They always seem to be happy when they see her. Janet always talks to the animals. I think that she loves her job, don't you?

Name ....

Reading Challenge

After reading "Janet, the Zookeeper," answer the following questions.

1. **Answer these questions with words from the story which contain the long ā sound. Write the answer on the lines below.**

   animals live in ____________________

   water was ____________________

2. **Which zoo animals do you think would like bananas?** ____________________

   ____

3. **What does listless mean? Put an X next to the correct answer.**

   _____ **A.** happy and excited

   _____ **B.** no energy, not happy

   _____ **C.** hungry and thirsty

4. **Fill in the blanks with a long vowel to complete the words. The words are in the story if you need help.**

___at	s__ __ds	c___ld	cl___an
c___ges	___ach	v___tamins	kn___w
k__ __per	sl__ __p	g___es	r___ght
gr___in	l___ke	k__ __p	d___n't
m___at	s___fe	spr___y	t___ke

5. **Name two things Janet has to do to take care of the animals.** ____________

   ____

6. **What is another name for a Zoo Doctor?** ______________________________

7. **Name one zoo animal that likes to live where it is warm and one that likes to live where it is cold.**

   warm ____________________ cold ____________________

Total Correct ________

"Sea" What You Can See

The sea is such a wonderful place to be. You can see all shapes, sizes and colors of fish. There are fish with stripes and fish with spikes. There are long skinny eels and large whales. There are bright, colorful fish and dull colored fish. There are fish that you need to stay away from, as well as fish you can swim along with.

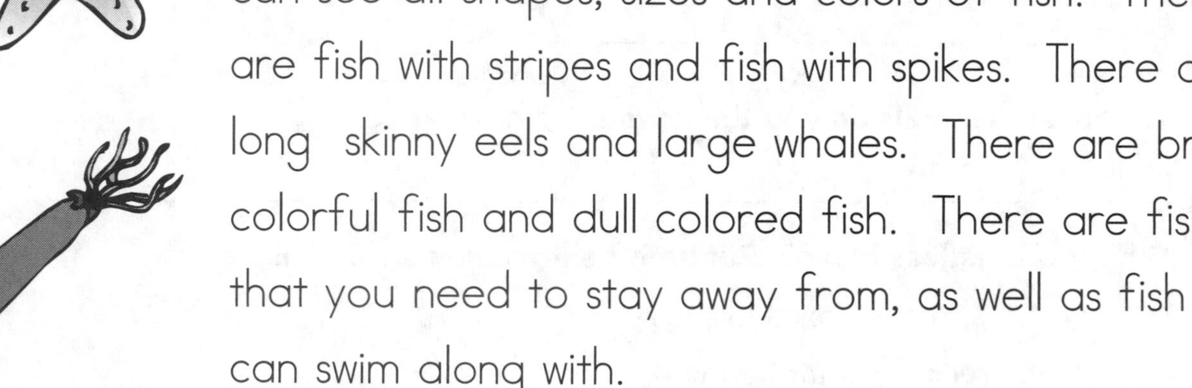

There are different kinds of plants in the sea, too. Some plants are okay to eat, others you better stay away from!

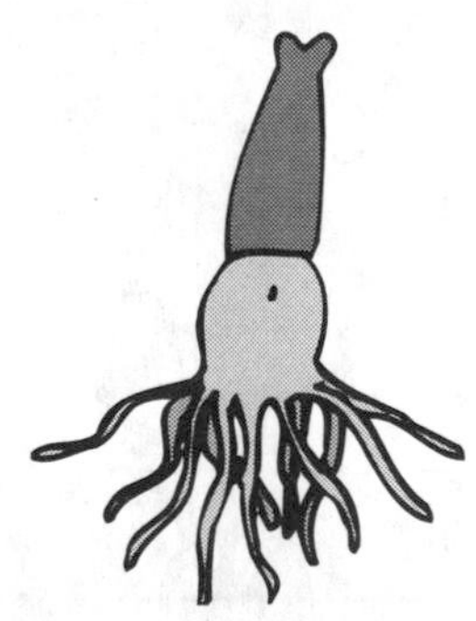

Some parts of the ocean can be light and bright. Down deep in the ocean it is very dark, making it very hard to see what lives there. The ocean's secrets are hidden away there.

Sea animals are some of the most interesting and unusual creatures at this depth. The starfish is not really a fish. It is a marine animal. It looks like a

star because of its arms. The sea cucumber is another animal of the sea. It is shaped like a cucumber but has ten tentacles at one end to help it get its food. The sea urchin is shaped like a ball covered with long sharp spines. It has five sharp teeth under its body.

Have you seen a sea peach? It is not a fruit but a kind of sea squirt. It has two openings, one for food, and the other to squirt out extra water that it does not need or want. Then there is my favorite, the sea anemone. The sea anemone looks like a flower. It can be pink, blue, green, red or a mixture of colors. It has a base, or foot, that connects itself to something solid while it waits for food to come swimming or floating by.

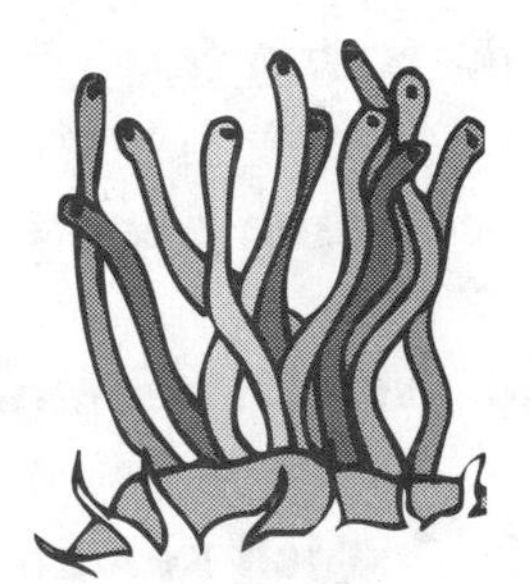

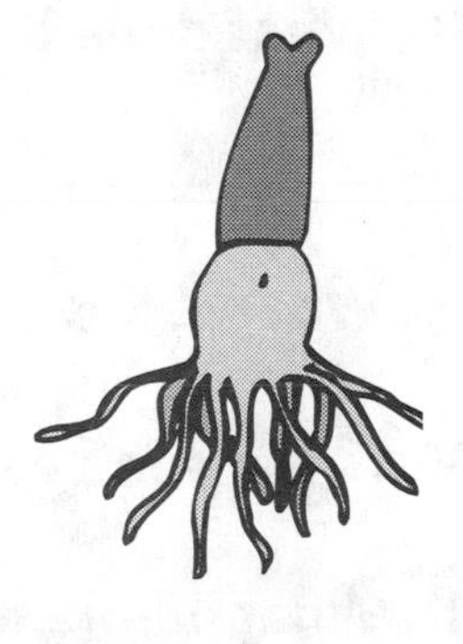

Come to the sea! Come to the sea, to see what you can see! Maybe I'll come along, too!

Name ______________________

READING CHALLENGE

After reading "Sea What You Can See," answer the following questions.

In questions 1-5, fill in the blanks correctly with the homonym from the word list below that matches the underlined word in each sentence. A homonym is a word having the same sound as another word, but which is both spelled differently and has a different meaning.

flour	sea	too
blew	eight	

1. **How far can you see out into the ______________________?**
2. **Even though the sky was blue, the wind ___________ very hard.**
3. **When I was making cookies, I got ______ all over the colorful flower print on my dress.**
4. **Sam ate ________ fish for his dinner.**
5. **I have been to the fish shop and I have to go to the shoe shop, ______.**
6. **Which sea animal looks like a flower? ______________________**
7. **Which sea animal looks like a star? ______________________**
8. **What does the sea urchin look like? ______________________**

    ____
9. **What word in the story rhymes with bright? ______________________**
10. **Is the sea peach a fruit for the other fish to eat? ______________________**
11. **What colors can a sea anemone be? ______________________**

    ____
12. **What very large animal lives in the sea? ______________________**

Total Correct ________

Did You Know?

Did you know that Weddel seals have to breathe air to live but can stay under water for an hour?

Did you know that wolves travel in packs, fish travel in schools and a pod is the name for a group of_whales?

Did you know that most sharks have 4 to 6 rows of teeth and some can have as many as 20 rows?

Did you know that mother deer and arctic hares are called does?

Did you know that baby hares are born with their eyes open and have fur, while baby rabbits do not?

Did you know that div–ing petrel birds can use their wings to fly right through waves and come up from the water flying?

Did you know that cold water is heavier than warm water, so that when ice melts, the cold water sinks down and runs along the bottom causing a cold current?

Did You Know? (continued)

Did you know that nine-tenths of all the ice on the earth is found on Antarctica's ice cap?

Did you know that for the first few months of their life, baby lobsters float near the surface of water?

Did you know that the word "school" came from the word meaning "spare time?"

Did you know that when an octopus is frightened, its skin turns bright red?

Did you know that algae is a seaweed, and that it makes its own food?

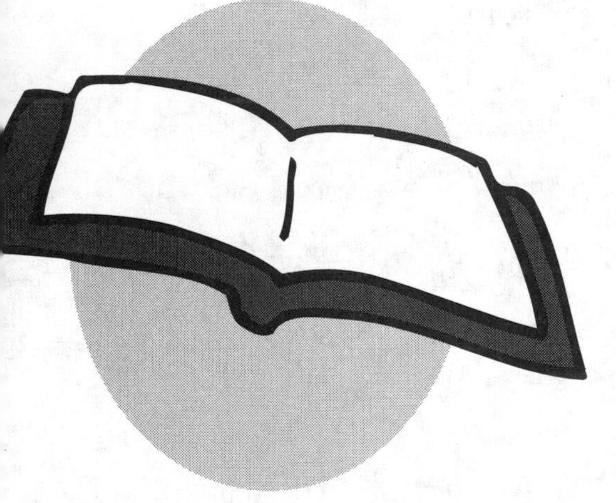

Did you know all or any of these things?

I knew some, but the others I read about in books. Interesting, huh? Let's read!

READING CHALLENGE

After reading "Did You Know?," answer the following questions.

Find these words in the word search and color them. Look for the words going up, down and diagonally. Some words can share the same letter.

weddel	wolves	whales	sharks
hares	rabbits	petrels	Antarctica
lobsters	octopus	algae	read
books			

```
b o o k s l p w h a l e s
q y m o x a a o u e s l e
b d f g h n s l j k o r y
a c d s f t i v p r i s z
z x e l i a m e n o e q x
y o z b o r p s q r y w p
d w b s e c y k a u w s e
m a o b c t g h f g e i t
r e a d n i r u s w d t r
g j l m o c t v h a d r e
a e a l g a e i a o e u l
b u k n p q i c r a l b s
m l s r s k t w k c b a v
s l o b s t e r s f g c q
f r z w p v o c t o p u s
```

Total Correct ________

Grandma's Dinner

Mom was planning to take dinner to Grandma's house. Grandma was sick in bed. She did not feel like fixing dinner. Mom said, "June and Zane, I need your help. I need you to go on an errand for me. Go to the store and get some salt and black pepper. I also need eggs to make a spice cake." Grandma's favorite cake is a spice cake with white frosting.

Zane and I walked down the street to the store. While we were walking, we past the flower shop. We saw a clown out front who was handing out fresh flowers! He waved to us, so we went over to visit. We told the clown we were going to bake a cake for our grandma because she was sick. He gave us a bunch of fresh flowers and told us to give them to our Grandma. We thanked the clown. We were very excited to give our beautiful present to Grandma.

We went on to the store and got the things we needed. Mom fixed the dinner and baked the cake for Grandma. We went to Grandma's house. Grandma got her dinner and favorite cake, plus a colorful bunch of beautiful flowers!

Name ....

READING CHALLENGE

After reading "Grandma's Dinner," answer the following questions.

1. **What is Grandma's favorite cake?** ____________________

2. **Who went to the store?** __________ **and** __________ **.**

3. **What did the children see on their way to the store?** ____________________

   ____

4. **Do you think Grandma enjoyed the dinner, cake and flowers?** ____________________

   ____

   Why or why not? ____________________

   ____

Write the words from the story that correctly fill in the blank below.

5. **A person who is your mother's or father's mother is your:** ____________________

6. **A meal in the evening is:** ____________________

7. **A way to move your body with your legs is to:** ____________________

8. **A black spice that goes on food:** ____________________

9. **A white seasoning that goes on food:** ____________________

10. **A colorful character, with a big nose, usually found at a circus** ____________________

Total Correct __________

MIGHTY DRAGONS

A long time ago, a boy named Elwood dreamed of slaying mighty dragons. In the land of Dirksville, anyone who is anyone had slayed at least one dragon. His father had slayed his first dragon when he was younger than Elwood. Elwood had heard his father tell stories of the mighty dragons all his life.

If the truth be told, Elwood was terribly afraid of anything larger than a dog. So you see, it was with great fear and trembling body that he set out to slay his first dragon.

He wandered in the forest of the dragons, hoping to find one fast asleep that he could slay. He didn't. He kept on walking. He became very tired and hungry. He stumbled upon a great palace. He knocked on the front door, and who should pull him inside, but a great, big, fierce, mighty dragon!

Now Elwood was mighty scared but he was not dumb. He replied shakily, "Is this the palace of the most great, most noble, most fierce of all the mighty dragons?"

Horace, the dragon, boasted that indeed it was. "Show me," replied a very scared Elwood. With that, Horace huffed and puffed and puffed and huffed until all the fire he had left was a

MIGHTY DRAGONS, continued

tiny little puff of smoke. Horace stomped and stamped and stamped and stomped angrily because he had no fire left. With all the stamping and stomping, the walls of the palace began to crack and crumble. With a loud explosion, the walls came tumbling down.

Elwood escaped just in the nick of time! He brought the people of Dirksville back to the palace to see how he had brought down a mighty dragon in his mighty castle! Three cheers for Elwood! Hip, hip, hurrah! Hip, hip, hurrah! Hip, hip, hurrah!

Name ....

READING CHALLENGE

After reading "Mighty Dragons," answer the following questions.

1. **What is the name of the land where Elwood lived?** ____________________

2. **"Anyone who is anyone had slayed at least one dragon" means (put an X next to the correct answer):**

   _____ **A.** Only grown up people had slayed dragons.

   _____ **B.** Slaying dragons is an important thing for people in Dirksville to do.

   _____ **C.** Only girls can slay dragons.

3. **Unscramble these words. If you need help, the words are in the story. The first letter of the word is underlined for you.**

   fdaair ____________________ ufefdp ____________________

   gdnora ____________________ ohubtgr ____________________

   leacap ____________________ cespdea ____________________

4. **Match the words by drawing a line to the correct name.**

   town Elwood

   boy Horace

   house Dirksville

   dragon palace

5. **Do you think Elwood is now one of the "anyone who is anyone" people in the town of Dirksville?** ____________________

   Why? ____________________

   ____

6. **Do you think Elwood was smart, or brave, or both smart and brave?**

   ____

Total Correct ________

Check Yourself

Page 9, Sam and Rab
1. mat: cat, hat, pat, bat, at, sat;
2. Rab, **3.** cap, hat, bag, bat;
4. Answers will vary but examples are: bag: tag, wag, jag, lag, sag, rag; tap: lap, map, sap, rap, slap, nap; tan: man, fan, can, pan, ran, van; **5.** He wanted to take a nap. **6.** picture.

Page 11, The Tan Rat
1. Answers will vary. Tax: Max, wax, fax. Some children could put jacks, packs or other "acks" words.
2. her hat, **3.** to get away from Pam,
4. tan, **5.** in a can, **6.** the man,
7. because Pam was tapping Tax, the rat, **8.** nab, **9.** Answers will vary. Examples: Give it to Pam for a pet. Take it to a zoo. Keep it himself.

Page 13, A Big Wig
1. pig, cat, frog, ram; **2.** tan pig, thin cat, big ram; **3.** Answers will vary. green, **4.** frog: log, jog, dog; **5.** fast, **6.** A. wig, pig; B. ram, bam; C. tip, zip; D. thin, pin; **7.** yes.

Page 15, Pig, Hen and Chicks
1. Tim, **2.** wheat, bugs, grass, seeds; Answers will vary. **3.** the pig, because he is running after the hen and her chicks. He is scaring them. **4.** in a pen; **5. A.** pen, **B.** book, **C.** sack, **D.** little; **6.** big and little, **7.** They had been running so much, they were tired.
8. ten, hen, pen.

Page 17, Meg, The Vet
1. a doctor for animals, **2.** pet and get, **3.** He has been sick and now he has no pep. **4.** yes, **5.** Answers will vary. They may be dirty from playing in the mud. They may have spilled a big bottle of milk. They make have gotten paint all over them. **6.** call: fall, tall, ball, mall, wall; **7.** yes, **8.** yes, **Why?** Because they are animals and Meg is a vet. **9.** mess, guess.

Page 19, Pups and Cub
1. cubs - bear, pups - dog, foal - horse, kitten - cat, calf - cow; **2.** B, **3.** Tom and Bill, **4.** a fox, **5.** cubs: tubs, rubs; pup: cup, up; **6.** So it would not hurt their cubs. Answers will vary.
7. Tom, Bill and Nan.

Page 21, I Wish
1. ă: all, what, had, can, fan, man, and, yams, ham, Mack, Jack; ĕ: hen, pen, sled, bed; ĭ: wish, fish, dish, in, ring, sing, ship, trip, chips, dips, with; ŏ: frog, on, log, fox, box, dog, hog, socks, locks, Tom, Mom; ŭ: cubs, tubs, pups, cups; **2.** story and picture.

Page 23, At the Pond
1. pictures, **2. A.** F, **B.** T, **C.** T, **D.** F, **E.** F, **F.** T.

Page 25, Pets Are Friends
1. everywhere, someday, understand, cannot; **2.** country, **3.** no,
4. The lady at the local store,
5. Lucky and Happy, **6.** sandwich, chips, carrots, apples, dog bones;
7. in the summer, **8** pups-dogs, small-little, friends-pals, talk-speak; **9.** C,

Page 27, Josh's Backpack
1. A. mascot, **B.** scissors, **C.** lion, **D.** pen, **2.** to show something of interest to your school class, **3.** books, box of crayons, soccer picture and cup, soccer ball, mascot or Thomas Team Tiger, three pencils and school tablet; **4.** Mr. Jacobs, **5.** yes, **6.** lunch box,

7. Answers will vary except there is no words in the story for k, u, v, x and z.

Page 29, It's Time
1. time: rhyme, dime, lime, slime, crime; **2.** Answers will vary, **3.** in-out, stay-come, here-there, worst-best, old-young, you-me, down-up, stop-go, bad-good; **4.** minute, hour, second, years, months, days, weeks;
5. Answers will vary.

Page 31, Move, Dance, Follow
1. dancing, chasing, waddling, frolicked, pecking, tip-toed, crawled, creeping; **2.** Monday **3.** 2, 1, 4, 3, 5; **4. A.** dancing, playing, quacking, watching; **B.** chasing, doing, pecking, waddling; **5. Crossed Out:** call, school, cave, can, candy, ducks, circle; **Circled:** prance, dance, cell, recess, cinder, circle.

Page 33, The Shipmate
1. James & Uncle Nate, **2.** on the lake, **3.** know, Nate, boat, time, keeper, used, James, sail, neat, ride, blue, soap; **long ā:** James, Nate, sail;
long ē: keeper, neat; **long ī:** ride, time;
long ō: boat, soap, know;
long ū: used, blue; **4.** He would keep James as his shipmate.

Page 35, Quiet Time
1. Not true: Quiet time is at night when everyone is asleep. **2.** believe, strange, animals, dream, outer;
3. fact, soon, animals, quiet, grown-ups.

Page 37, Boats and Acorns
1. squirrels, Ellen, squirrels, Garn, squirrels; **2.** boats, fun, look, made, rocks, more, green, bush; **3.** to eat in the winter, **4.** blue and green,
5. wood and paper, **6.** Answers will vary.

Page 39, Firemen Know
1. A. assembly, B. a stack of hay that cows can eat, C. something just happens without making it happen,
2. Being safe from fire. **3.** Stop what you are doing, drop to the ground or floor and roll around. **4.** animal, match, child, **5.** Answers will vary.

Page 41, What's For Lunch?
1. nobody, **2.** really, lunch, scramble, desperate; **3.** no bread, **4.** no eggs,
5. can opener, **6.** Answers will vary.
7. at, or, chat, fun, hat, us, nut, has, far, war, car, tar, four, hunch, tan, slat, half, two, ton, won, cart, launch, warf.

Page 43, Space Travel
1. two, grade, world, thrilled, sailed, ship; **2.** dream, into space, learn things, planets; **3.** traveled, traveling, dreamed, dreaming, listened, listening, finished, finishing; **4.** Answers will vary.

Page 45, World of Color
1. Answers will vary. **2. A.** don't,
B. why, sky; **C.** found, cows, around;
D. rainbows; **3.** color, read, real, rose;
4. Answers will vary.

Page 47, Hide and Seek
1. C, **2.** Dad: socks, Julie: dust rag, Mom: spoon, **3.** play, call, decide, look, start, ask, mix, use; **4. A.** no - white, **B.** no - looked, **C.** yes, **D.** yes, **E.** no - over, **F.** no - let's.

CHECK YOURSELF, continued

Page 49, The Ranch
1. hand - land, go - so, range - change, cattle - battle, other - mother, cook - look; **2.** hay, oats, corn, grass; **3. A.** Queed, **B.** Dave, ranch, **C.** sold; **4.** go to town to dance and be with other people, **5.** D, **6.** Rafe & Queed.

Page 51, Wild Animals for Benjamin
1. bears and buffaloes, **2.** in Yellowstone National Park, **3.** big, **4.** wild - tame, sharp - dull, strong - weak, him - her, went - came, lots - few; **5.** A, **6.** 3, 1, 2; **7.** animal crackers.

Page 53, Sampson, the Robot
1. a robot, a boy; **2.** dance, sing, cook, do chores outside and inside, read; **3.** Sampson wandered out by himself. **4.** at the library, **5. A.** open area, **B.** people who travel in space, **C.** wonderful, **D.** to hunt for new things or places, **E.** answered, **F.** a place to find books, **G.** to find new things or places; **6.** Answers will vary. **Examples:** so, Sam, bat, boat, sat, that, nap, spam, son, pen, pan, map, some soap, bear, hat, toe, toes, boot, boots, rat, man, bet, same, some, am, he, hen, set, ramp, stamp, stamps;

Page 56, Barney Bear
1. He could not sleep and it was winter, or he could not hibernate with the rest of his family because he was not tired. **2.** In the forest, **3.** laughing, **4.** John Skunk, **5. A.** T, **B.** T, **C.** T, **D.** F, **E.** T, **F.** F; **6. Circled: A.** shouted - yelled, **B.** bashful - shy, **C.** quiet - hushed, **D.** hibernating - sleeping.

Page 59, Aunt Jenny's Forest
1. 4, 2, 5, 3, 1; **2.** running very fast, **3.** tall green trees and the colorful flowers, **4.** He wanted to see more things in the forest, and by going slow and quiet, he could. **5. Circled:** close, safe, told, see, time, bee, wild, way; **Box around:** nest, long, them, left, him, summer, went, plant.

Page 61, What's In a Cake?
1. ask - task, told - gold, milk - silk, bake - take, bake - cake, wrong - long; **2.** four, **3.** flour, vanilla, shortening, milk; **4. A.** 2,1; **B.** 1, 2; **5.** it's, don't, what's, haven't, you're, I'm, we're, let's; **6.** Answers will vary.

Page 64, Garden Mouse and House Mouse
1. M, R, R, M, R; **2.** house - mouse, sickly - quickly, crunch - munch, beets - streets, Gus - bus, Rome - home; **3.** buses, friends, mice, cookies, roads, boxes; **4.** to explore, **5.** tiny bites, **6.** most of one day.

Page 67, Camp Sage
Across: 1. five, **2.** skyscraper, **5.** crafts, **6.** letter. **Down: 1.** fast, **3.** country, **4.** start

Page 70, Backyard Camping
1. Brian, Tommy; **2.** snacks, **3.** tuna fish sandwiches, potato chips, cookies and milk; **4.** Tiger, **5.** shaky voice, **6. A.** monster, radio, bottle, **B.** camping, meow, flashlight, **C.** closer, garage, pulled, **D.** sandwich, backyard, potato, **E.** equipment, decided, pajamas; **7.** in their backyard.

Page 73, Little Toad

l a p o m t o a d s x t j r y i n i o
b f f c g d h e o i k m o a q s u w x
z r l k m o i e g y u z x b a h b y m
w o r a b d j k m n o p q b v w x y z
m g i o v m t s p a b c l i n a v t j
s v t c o w u l i m a d b t f s h i o
r t v a x a c e g i k y p q b l o x m
m k a t b f o x y d u c k s t s r r e
x z y m p q b c a n o s i t u d s f g
s v d j k l u b e e h e a o n c e d p
f o f i s h m u v x s i w z a r c i y

1. fox. It is on the same line as ducks.

Page 76, Gardens

1. the pet dog, **2.** any three of the following: along fences, in pots, window boxes, on bushes, by sidewalks, in the pond; **3. Circle:** potatoes, turnips, parsnips; **4.** flowers & vegetables, **5.** long $\bar{i}$: I, time, Spike, idea, while, sidewalks, bright, night, decided, might; long $\bar{e}$: decided, she, we'll, he, money, seeds, we, people's, green, beans, peas, beets, even, weeds, seen, eating, season; **6.** Answers will vary.

Page 79, Janet, the Zookeeper

1. A. cages, B. sprayed, **2.** monkey & apes, **3.** B, **4.** eat, seeds, cold, clean, cages, each, vitamins, know, keeper, sleep, goes, right, grain, like, keep, don't, meat, safe, spray, take; **5.** feed them, keep the animals healthy, clean their cages, give them water to drink, make sure their cages are at the right temperature for them; **6.** vet or veterinarian, **7.** Answers will vary.

Page 82, "Sea" What You Can See

1. see - sea, **2.** blue - blew, **3.** flowers - flour, **4.** ate - eight, **5.** to - too, **6.** sea anemone, **7.** starfish, **8.** shaped like a ball, covered with long sharp spines. It has sharp teeth under its body. **9.** bright - light, **10.** no **11.** pink, blue, green, red or a mixture of colors; **12.** whale.

Page 85, Did You Know

Page 87, Grandma's Dinner

1. spice, **2.** June and Zane, **3.** a clown, **4.** Answers will vary. **5.** grandma, dinner, walk, pepper, salt, clown.

Page 91, Mighty Dragons

1. Dirksville, **2.** B, **3.** afraid, puffed, dragon, brought, palace, escaped; **4.** Elwood - boy, Horace - dragon, Dirksville - town, palace - house; **5.** yes, because he has slayed a dragon, **6.** smart and brave,

www.rainbowbridgepub.com